C000108840

THE
CHANGING
THAMES

BRIAN EADE

The
History
Press

This volume is dedicated with love to my wife Louise.

THE LOCK

Chains chink against the wall,
slimy green algae covering them.
Drops of water
suspended.
A pervasive stench of rotting wood.

Sunlight on swirly rainbows.
Diesel does look pretty in the sun.
The hot wall pushing back;
space closing in.

Silt laden brown water returns,
bringing dirty twigs and oily vegetation.
The water's surface
flecked with yellow foam.

Tiny noises of moving ice,
creaking, cracking.
Spider web glistening
and frost hanging
in white ribbons
from the cold iron chains.

First published 2009

The History Press
The Mill, Brimscombe Port
Stroud, Gloucestershire, GL5 2QG
www.thehistorypress.co.uk

British Library Cataloguing in Publication Data.
A catalogue record for this book is available from the British Library.

ISBN 978 0 7509 4779 4

Typesetting and origination by The History Press
Printed in Great Britain
Title page photograph: Author and mother paddling at Clifton Lock, 1958.

CONTENTS

ACKNOWLEDGEMENTS

This volume would not have been possible without the generous help of those listed below. I am delighted to acknowledge their time, help and interest with photographs and information. I have also been given unprecedented access to private land and other areas in order to obtain the modern views and would like to thank these individuals as well. While every effort has been made to trace the owners or copyright holders of the photographs, some errors may have crept in. If this is the case, corrections will be made in later editions. Barbara Aldridge, Geoff Aldridge, Beverly Bagnell, David Beasley, Adam Benge, Caroline Benson, Duncan Birtles, Brett Bodiam, Stewart Boik, Tricia Buckingham, Brian Butcher, Dr Jonathan Brown, Steve Capel-Davies, Liam Challis, Colin Chestnut, Ken Clarke, Michael Cole, Louise Cooper, Delyth Davies, Marcia Dieppe, Janet Dudman, Steve Drewett, Keith Edwards, Philip Emerton, Ray Evans, Leigh Fenton, Jonathan Finch, Hilary Fisher, Dennis Fogden, Roger French, Veronica Giles, Dr Malcolm Graham, Joe Green, Colin Harris, David Hemingway, Geoff Horsnell, Igor Hotez, Steve Hooper, Fiona Kemp, Steve Long, Bob Mainwaring, Timmy Mallett, David Mannal, Sarah Markham, James Marshall, Howard Miatt, Nathan Murray, Justin Nelson, Steve Newman, Graham Parlour, Colin Reynolds, Ian Richards, Giles Robinson, Michael Roe, David Rogers, Gwyneth Rogers, Peter Scott, Paul Sims, Andrew Shacknove, Paul Shrimpton, Ian Smith, the Revd Michael Smith, Sam Smith, Jeannette Stuart, Pete Svendsen, Lesley Talbot, Annie Tatham-Mannal, Catherine Taylor, Susan Taylor, Ken Townsend, Arthur Vanson, Simon Wenham, John Williams, Gaius Wyncoll.

A special mention must go to Dawn Greening-Steer, archivist with the Environment Agency, without whose help many of these images could not have been included.

The Bodleian Library, University of Oxford, Centre for Oxfordshire Studies, Colourbox Techunique, Compleat Anglers Hotel, D & R Engineering, Environment Agency, Hounslow Local Studies Centre, Museum of English Rural Life, Open Spaces Society, Oxford Cruisers Ltd, Red Bull Marine, River & Rowing Museum, River Thames Society, Runnymede Hotel, The Riverside Restaurant, Salters Steamers, Two Brewers, Walton Marine, Wilts & Berks Canal Trust.

INTRODUCTION

Left to its own devices, a river will flow seawards in any direction, restricted mainly by geological features. Hills, rocky outcrops, a fallen tree or a build up of gravel can force a change in its direction. As a naturally flowing river, the River Thames would frequently breach its banks in winter and often dry up during long hot summers.

Constant flooding would lead to riverside meadows becoming very fertile as deposits of river sediment built up over each season. These nutrient-rich deposits made for lush meadows ideal for grazing livestock and growing crops, and many settlements sprung up around these meadows as a result. There was little river management for hundreds of years; the earliest attempts occurred around the time of Edward the Confessor in 1066, who ordered that some mills and fish weirs be destroyed to provide better navigation. Further changes to the river occurred when King Richard I sold off his interest in the Thames to fund his crusades in about 1197. King James I passed an act in 1605 authorising the appointment of the Oxford–Burcot Commissioners to investigate and improve the state of the Thames near Oxford.

The Thames in this area was in disarray, with shoals and shallows causing huge problems for barge operators who would sometimes have to unload their cargoes and continue by horse and cart; a slow and costly delay. In about 1632, the Commission instigated the building of the first pound locks on the Thames at Iffley, Sandford and Swift Ditch at Abingdon. Iffley has a few remnants of the original lock, upstream of the existing weir, and little else apart from an information plaque. Sandford was filled in sometime after 1836 and a new lock was built alongside. Swift Ditch, above Abingdon lock, has survived virtually intact with only the gates missing and some growth around the walls. There were however, earlier forms of lock before the building of these three pound locks. Flash locks or weirs were simply crudely made dams across the river with removable parts. Craft wishing to pass downstream would flash down on the released water. Going up against the stream required a lot more effort and craft were either towed or winched. These flash locks were frequently named after the men who built or owned them; Skinner's, Harper's, Ridge's, Swithun's, King's, Day's and Hart's. These crude structures caused lengthy delays and wasted vast amounts of water. King's and Day's have survived as pound locks but not in the same locations as the original flash weirs.

Further acts relating to the management of the Thames were instigated in an Act of 1751 under King George II which saw the formation of the Thames Navigation Commission who took control of the river down to Staines. Below Staines was the responsibility of the Corporation of the City of London.

Under the Thames Navigation Commission several bylaws were put in place, including one relating to the obstruction of the river, which read thus:

That no Person whosoever, shall erect any new Bucks, or Weirs, or drive, or affix any Piles or Stakes, or make any Hedge or plant any Willows or Osiers, in the said Rivers, or take away any of the Soil of the said Rivers, without the permission and consent in writing, of seven or more of the said Commissioners, assembled at a General Meeting first had and obtained; and that no Person shall throw any Stones, Chalk, Rubbish, Soil or other matter whatsoever, into the said Rivers, as to obstruct, impede, annoy or otherwise injure the free Navigation thereon.

This was just one of the thirty or so bylaws, rules, orders or regulations relating to navigation that the Commissioners instigated.

As the management of the Thames gradually improved, more barges carrying goods were navigating up and down the river. These barges had to be hand-towed by gangs of men known as 'halers' (literally haulers). It could take upwards of fifty men to haul a fully laden barge upstream, time consuming and very hard work. These men were often of such bad character that the Commissioners added another bylaw specific to their behaviour:

> Whereas frequent Complaints have been made by Gentlemen and others navigating on said rivers for pleasure, or otherwise, that they have been exposed to and suffered Obstructions, Threats and Nuisances from Barge masters, Costbearers and their Crews; In order to prevent the like in future, if any Barge master, Costbearer, or their Crews or other Persons navigating the said rivers shall obstruct, hinder, or interrupt any Person navigating on the same, or molest, insult, threaten or abuse, any such Person, the Person so offending, shall be subject and liable to the penalty hereinafter set, for breach of these bye laws.

Penalties or fines were severe for these breaches and ran from 20s up to £20, even £50 for the more serious offences. It is little wonder that horses became increasingly popular to carry out this work, as they were obviously less likely to obstruct, hinder, molest, insult, threaten or abuse!

The Barge masters and Cost bearers mentioned in the early Commissioners bylaws had to contend with many obstructions and the worst of these were mills and their owners. In 1086, a complete survey of England was taken – commonly referred to as the Domesday Book. This survey recorded over five thousand watermills in England. Monks and millers built mills and fish weirs astride the Thames, all aimed at extracting food, power or money in the form of tolls. Generally speaking, the monks were more interested in being self-sufficient, whereas the commercial millers were hard-nosed and often ruthless businessmen. They ruled the Thames with an iron fist and imposed exorbitant tolls on barge masters and others to pass their mills. Owing to the small amount of gradient fall of the Thames, millers would allow the water to build up excessively in order to turn their wheels. Delays were frequent and fighting would often break out at these delays and obstructions, with the mill owner refusing passage until a time that suited him. It is interesting to note that many of these former mill sites are now occupied by some of the most expensive properties in the United Kingdom.

By far the greatest number of changes to the River Thames commenced after the formation of the Thames Conservancy in 1857. During their reign, the Thames Conservancy undertook enormous improvement projects: lock building and mechanisation, making lock cuts, removing old flash weirs, building new weirs and dredging channels, all until 1974 when they were finally disbanded.

With major engineering works completed, including huge flood relief channels, it is difficult to determine the future changes for the River Thames. Improved flood management is the most likely change as the summer floods of July 2007 could be the start of a worrying trend for flash-flooding.

Despite high-level assertions that the River Thames is self-scouring, perhaps the Environment Agency could reintroduce river dredging where appropriate? The benefits could be two-fold, increased river depths and increased bank heights. On a constantly changing river, surely this is one lesson from the past that may signal a positive change for the future of Old Father Thames?

1

THAMES HEAD TO ABINGDON

The numerous changes that have occurred upstream of Culham Lock were mainly navigation improvements, chiefly the removal of the old flash locks. Eaton Hastings, Eynsham, Kings and Medley have all been dismantled. At Eynsham and Kings the old flash locks have been converted into weirs, while Eaton Hastings and Medley have been completely removed. The mill at Sandford has been demolished to make way for housing, while at Osney the ancient mill has been allowed to gradually decay. Iffley Mill simply burnt down, the cause of the fire unknown.

In their heyday, wharves at Lechlade, Abingdon and Oxford were busy with barge traffic; today these locations have changed considerably. The old warehouse at Lechlade has become a pub, Abingdon wharf is now a popular place to feed the swans, while at Oxford the ubiquitous 'luxury riverside' housing developments were inevitable. Mysteriously at Oxford, the River Thames changes its name to Isis and even cartographers have been duped into marking maps as 'River Thames or Isis' here. What relevance does an ancient Egyptian Goddess have to do with an English river?

Two elegantly dressed ladies photographed by Henry Taunt at Thames Head, date unknown. The Thames rises from the many underground springs in this area, including this one. For most times of the year this particular spring does not show water above ground. Despite this, it is still designated as the official source. (*Environment Agency*)

The author's wife Louise at the source, September 2008. The most significant difference from the earlier view has been the installation of a stone to mark the source after the removal of the Old Father Thames statue to nearby St John's Lock. (*Author*)

Looking across the river to Park End wharf at Lechlade during the flooding in about 1906. The building on the left was once an eighteenth-century storage barn for this busy wharf. With the opening of the nearby Thames & Severn Canal in 1789, commercial barge traffic greatly increased bringing coal, fruit, salt, cheese and copper to the many wharves here. On an 1859 map, there were at least five wharves noted, some of which dated back to the thirteenth century. The shed to the right of the view was owned by Hicks where there were 'boats for hire'. (*Ken Townsend*)

Photographed in 2007, the former Park End wharf location now has an antique centre, a marina and bed & breakfast accommodation. The eighteenth-century storage barn seen in the previous view has become a popular riverside pub, but there is virtually no commercial traffic here apart from the hire boats. Ha'penny Bridge on the right of the view was originally named Town Bridge but soon adopted the nick name from the cost of the toll to cross it. The bridge was freed of all tolls by 1875. (*Author*)

Looking upstream towards St John's Lock with the spire of St Lawrence's church in the distance; possibly a Henry Taunt photograph, judging by the composition and style but not marked as such. Named after the local priory of 1250, St John's Lock was built on the site of an earlier flash weir of 1775. The cottage on the right of the view was built in 1830 and demolished in 1905. (*Author*)

It took several attempts to capture this view of St John's Lock in 2007. In order to photograph this, it was necessary to climb on to a towpath handrail and lean out with only one hand holding a weak-looking branch! The lock has remained virtually unchanged, while everything else around it has altered significantly. A pump out station, toilets and a visitor facility are to the left of the towpath which has been upgraded along with improved bank protection. The lock house is now on the left-hand bank replacing an earlier twin-roofed cottage dating from about 1905. (*Author*)

Looking downstream to the new Buscot weir under construction in 1979. This weir was unique in that it was constructed first, then connected to the main channel later. The original weir is still in place along with the old lock cottage dating from the eighteenth century. This much older cottage had 'fish stews' (ponds stocked with fish) situated underneath it. Above this cottage is Brandy Island, the site of a former brandy distillery and rumours persist about casks of brandy sunk near here to avoid Customs duty. (*Environment Agency*)

Less than thirty years later, Buscot weir looks like it has always been here with riverside trees and vegetation softening the banks. However, the left-hand bank has suffered some significant bank erosion at the end of the steel pilings; the scouring action of the river has undermined the bank. In the distance, the footbridge carrying the Thames Path can be seen. (*Author*)

A 1926 photograph of the former flash weir at Eaton Hastings. Sometimes referred to as Hart's weir, this is one of several flash weirs which were all removed by 1937. For some time the weir keeper doubled up as landlord of the nearby Anchor Inn. This situation was not tolerated for long and certainly ended when the inn was destroyed by fire in 1970. There were also two large water wheels situated here which pumped irrigation water up to a reservoir at nearby Buscot Park for Robert Campbell's intensive farming experiment of 1863. (*Environment Agency*)

Eaton Hastings weir site photographed in 2007. The flash weir has been replaced with an elegant footbridge and mature trees hide the far bank. There are no foundations or any other evidence of the small cottage in the previous view. A small part of the Anchor Inn remains, used as storage for a local boat club. (*Author*)

Looking upstream towards the pillbox at the head of Grafton Lock, 1950s. During the Second World War the River Thames formed a natural defendable line should the Germans have succeeded with their invasion plans. Along the river banks there are numerous pillboxes as well as tank traps and gun emplacements. Because they were built to withstand bombs, they are notoriously difficult to demolish and some could now be considered as historic monuments. In about 1789, this lock was referred to as Days Wear or New Lock, although the lock was in fact a flash lock. A new pound lock was finally opened to boat traffic in 1896. (*Author*)

Grafton Lock in 2007 looks much the same, apart from extensive tree growth. The wooden lock office has gone, replaced by one out of sight at the opposite end of the lock. The coffee grinder sluices have been replaced and the lock steps have guard rails around them. The aforementioned pillbox was demolished at a later date, further details of which could not be found. A 'Lock Unmanned' sign was in evidence during my visit. This could be the likely scenario at some of the more remote locks. (*Author*)

Looking downstream to Radcot Lock, date unknown. Thames historian Fred Thacker refers to a weir at Radcot called Beck's in1746 but only as a fishing weir. It was called Harpers in 1866, demolished in 1868 and a new lock and weir constructed in 1892, after the purchase of the necessary land for £300. (*Philip Emerton*)

Radcot Lock looking downstream in the summer of 2007. In 1980, it was discovered that the old lock house in the previous view was suffering from subsidence. Six years later the bungalow just visible in this view was ready for occupation. Note the two silver umbrellas at the head and tail of the lock for sun protection. (*Author*)

Rushey weir photographed across the weir pool *c*. 1908. The lock was built of stone in about 1790. (*Ken Townsend*)

The same view nearly 100 years later and the effects of erosion can be seen clearly as the action of the water has scoured away huge amounts of the riverbank from the weir pool. (*Author*)

Northmoor Lock, seen in this 1950s view, only just succeeded in having this name as it was originally due to be named Appleton Lock after the much closer village. There were flash weirs in this vicinity variously named after the owners Ark, Rudges and Hart's, a name which appears in many Thames locations. (*Mary Clarke Collection*)

Northmoor Lock photographed from about the same position in 2007 looks almost the same as the earlier view. The lock keeper here asked a Dutch boater and his wife about what he thought was a hire boat. 'Just picked her up then?' he enquired. The man was very angry. 'How dare you!' he spluttered. 'We've been married seven years!' (*Author*)

Originally named Babbelak, the ferry at Bablock Hythe has been operating since 1212. In about 1855, a private proposal to replace the ferry with a bridge was abandoned after fierce opposition from the Earl of Abingdon who was concerned for his revenue from nearby Swinford Toll Bridge. The ferryboat was originally pulled across the river by a rope but this was considered a hazard to navigation and was replaced with a chain along the riverbed in 1894. Four years later a rope was in use again but reverted to a chain at the Thames Conservancy's insistence. By 1920 the rope had returned and remained until 1960 when the ferry ceased to operate. (*Author*)

A 2007 photograph of the Bablock Hythe ferry site. The former Chequers Inn has been renamed the Ferryman Inn. This was one of the most difficult new views to take and this is as close to the original as could be achieved owing to trees and long undergrowth. There have been recent rumours of a pedestrian foot crossing at this site, yet to come to fruition. (*Author*)

Looking downstream to Pinkhill Lock, 1926. This lock was referred to by Henry Taunt as Pinkle. The pound lock here was constructed in 1790, replacing the former flash lock owned and maintained by local dignitary, Lord Harcourt. (*Environment Agency*)

Pinkhill Lock photographed in 2007 from approximately the same position as in 1926, from a boardwalk above the lock. Bank erosion and vegetation has changed the view considerably making a similar photograph difficult. It is heartening to note the many mature trees. The old lock house was replaced in 1932 by the one seen in this view. (*Author*)

Like most Thames bridges, Swinford Bridge (seen here in the 1950s) was preceded by a ferry which in turn was preceded by a dangerous ford. Swine-ford perhaps? William Blackstone, business advisor to the Earl of Abingdon, cleverly included a clause in the act relating to construction of the toll bridge that ensured that the tolls would be for the 'Earl, his heirs and assigns forever.' An attempt was made to buy out the rights from the Earl in 1929, but at £100,000 this was deemed far too expensive. (*Unknown*)

Swinford Toll Bridge photographed one Saturday in 2007. An estimated three million vehicles use this bridge each year. The narrow bridge and the collection of tolls causes long and frustrating delays for many motorists. It took considerable time to obtain this photograph, as it was far too dangerous to step out into the road to shoot the exact view! (*Author*)

King's weir was once owned by nearby Godstow Abbey, in about 1156 under a grant by Reynold St Valery. King's weir was also mentioned in surveys of 1636 and 1765 but was excluded in 1841. In 1791, the weir was owned by the Duke of Marlborough who, for some reason, failed to collect his tolls. It is seen here in 1926, a year before the new pound lock was built on a virgin site. The old flash pass had a single pair of gates alongside a rack and pinion-operated weir. With this old flash weir situated on a tight sweep of the river, the new lock made navigation easier in high water conditions. (*Environment Agency*)

King's weir photographed from Pixey Mead in 2007. The earlier paddle and rymer arrangement have been replaced with electric gates, apart from the small overflow on the left. Remnants of the old boat slide can still be found to the left of the weir and the old lock hut has gone, with a Scout hut taking its place. Recently, a boater broke her leg at the lock; the lock keeper ran to his shed looking for a makeshift splint. Unable to find wood the right length, he ran back out with a long length of wood and a saw to cut it down. Cue screams from the lady thinking her leg was about to be amputated! (*Author*)

Looking upstream towards Godstow Lock, date unknown, with some of the nunnery visible to the centre of the view. Godstow Lock was built in 1790 at the lower end of a new cut excavated across the graveyard of this nunnery. Stones from the nunnery were taken in 1862 to enlarge the nearby Trout Inn, parts of which date back to 1133. Godstow Lock was completely rebuilt in 1924. (*Environment Agency*)

Godstow Lock in 2007, showing signs of serious bank erosion compared to the older view. Just visible in the background are what is left of the nunnery; this too has suffered damage from the elements. (*Author*)

Medley weir was one of the last operational flash weirs to be removed during the Thames Conservancy's Upper Thames Improvement Scheme. Like many of this type of weir there was a timetable for the release of water or 'flash' upon which craft could pass through. Here it was on Tuesdays and Fridays, whereas at Eynsham weir, it was on Mondays and Thursdays. The second weir to the right of this view controlled the flow of water into the ancient navigation channel through Oxford. (*MS. Top. Oxon d. 502, fol 55 Minn Coll. Neg. 21/3 Bodleian Library*)

Medley weir site, photographed in 2007. The flash weir was removed in 1928 along with some extensive dredging below Godstow Lock, all part of the aforementioned Upper Thames Improvement Scheme. The former lock cottage on the left is now in private ownership and parts of the old weir are still visible underwater. (*Author*)

Looking upstream to Osney Lock, date unknown. Built for £50 by convicts from Oxford Castle and opened in 1790, this lock owes its existence to the monks of Osney Abbey. In order to turn their waterwheels, these monks engineered the Thames to flow in this direction rather than the ancient channel that passed directly through Oxford city and past the castle. (*Ken Townsend*)

The 2007 view of Osney Lock is only slightly different at first glance, yet the lock is now hydraulically powered. There is a new lock house, an engineering facility and a navigation office behind it as well as a recently constructed towpath bridge. (*Author*)

Looking downstream to Folly Bridge, Oxford, date unknown. To the left of the view are the waterworks and in the background the Head of the River pub. There was once a weir between these waterworks and the head of the island with the old navigation channel to the right through a small lock. (*Author*)

Looking downstream to Folly Bridge in July 2007. The Head of the River pub is still there, hidden by trees. The waterworks have been demolished and replaced with flats. The freak floods in July 2007 claimed this narrow boat which was moved against advice and came to grief at the head of the island. It remained afloat for a few days and then partially sank; a stark warning for the unwary and an expensive recovery operation. (*Author*)

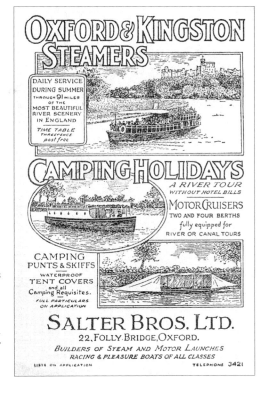

An early advertisement for Salter's steamers taken from a 1920s River Thames guide. Salter's steamers was started by boat building brothers John and Stephen Salter in 1858, the year they moved to Oxford to take over Isaac King's boat building business at Folly Bridge. As may be seen from this advert, they operated a regular steamer service, hired out camping punts and skiffs and offered camping holidays. (*Author*)

A modern advert for Salter's steamers that includes a website address and one of the old steamers. The company still operates steamers from Folly Bridge, albeit a less frequent service with diesel-powered steamers. Many of the former boat building premises have been sold off in recent years to make way for flats or apartments. (*Salter's Steamers Limited*)

Looking downstream from Folly Bridge, Oxford, date unknown. The photograph was probably taken during Eights Week as both the banks and college barges are packed with spectators. Moored on the left bank is a paddle steamer whose name remains elusive. Slightly downstream is a pontoon owned by D.A. Talboys who had 'boats to let & for sale'. (*Author*)

Eights Week in May 2008. Gone are the college barges, pontoons and paddle steamers yet the racing remains the same. Because the Thames is not wide enough here (unlike Henley) for side-by-side racing, the college eights have to 'bump' each other out of the heats. The eights start one and a half lengths apart in divisions of thirteen. The aim is to become 'Head of the River' that is, top of the first division. However, there must be something amiss in the Mathematics department of Oxford University, for the week only lasts four days and the eights have nine people in them! (*Author*)

Two navvies digging in the mud as part of the building of Iffley Lock. In 1923 work commenced on a new lock at Iffley and a realignment of the main channel. This project involved blocking and draining a huge pool of water which is where these workmen are working on the invert of the new lock chamber. (*Environment Agency*)

A 2008 view of Iffley Lock showing the completed 1924 lock and house. Sadly, this lock has had difficulties with local troublemakers in recent years and an exclusion zone was set up around the lock and weir. Closed-circuit cameras are in evidence in the area and at one point the lock keeper was issued with an anti-stab vest. (*Author*)

Looking from Iffley village towards the old lock at Iffley in about 1922. An 1875 map of this lock shows a ferry at the head of the island. This ferry was used for the transportation of coffins over the river avoiding the halfpenny toll by the mill; payment of this toll was said to establish a right of way. Roman Denarii and Saxon coins have also been discovered in the river below this lock. (*Mary Clarke Collection*)

A 2007 photograph of lots of trees! Hard to believe that this was once the Iffley Lock site. The lock that we see today opened in 1924 on the other side of these trees, the water in this view is now the weir stream passing through and over remnants of the 1632 pound lock. All that remains visible of the original lock is some of the ancient stonework at the head of the current weir channel. In 1885, locals petitioned for the removal of the mill, lock and weir because of low river levels in the reach above this lock. (*Author*)

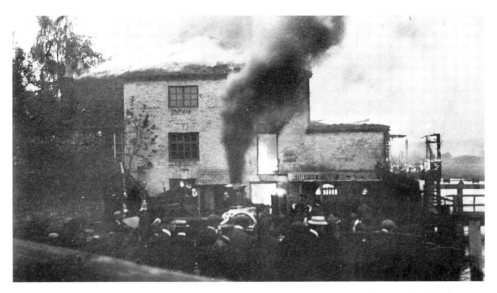

The caption on this postcard reads 'Fire at Iffley Mill, Oxford May 20th 1908'. All other references to this fire place the date on 27 May. Perhaps it took a week to burn down? It is certainly well ablaze here with smoke pouring both from the mill roof itself as well as the traction engine's funnel. It is unusual to have a view not taken from below the mill looking upstream. (*Ken Townsend*)

The site of Iffley Mill photographed in 2007 from approximately the same position. Although there is little to see of the mill and there are yet more trees, the site remains virtually as it was after the 1908 fire. Many other Thames mill sites have been turned into luxury riverside accommodation. (*Author*)

An old view of the Swan Hotel at Rose Island, Kennington, probably taken before 1870. In 1597, this property was connected with the Knights Templar from nearby Sandford and the island was referred to as St Michael's Island. In 1883 the pub was owned by Morlands brewery who sold it for £500 six years later to rival brewers Morrells. The lowest point of the house is higher than the meadows on the opposite bank and the house has only occasionally flooded. However, in the 1920s, the pub landlord Thomas Hawkins strapped two chairs to his feet to use as impromptu waders to walk out of his flooded gardens! (*Environment Agency*)

The former Swan Hotel at Kennington, photographed in 2007. Perhaps it was the camera used in the previous photograph but the three pointed roofs appear wider. There is an addition to the left of the building added after 1870. The banks are now concrete with a plea for a slower passage of vessels. Gone is the ferry boat and steps that would bring drinkers to the pub; traces of the landing place on the opposite bank may still be seen. The house is now in private ownership. (*Author*)

The Kings Arms Hotel in this view was converted from a malthouse used by Sandford Mill. It is likely that Sandford takes its name from sandy ford, referring to an earlier river crossing and the mill here dates back to about 1100 when it was owned by local monks for making bread. The Knights Templar owned the mill early in the fourteenth century when it was used for grinding corn. In 1520, it was let for £12 per annum, rent which also included a 'fish weir and lok'. The 'lok' would have been a flash lock as the pound lock was not constructed until 1632. The mill eventually closed on Christmas Eve 1982, having survived for over 800 years. (*Mary Clarke Collection*)

The Kings Arms photographed in 2007, virtually unchanged from the earlier view apart from the bank protection, the vanishing ivy and the picket fence. The nearby Sandford Mill has gone, replaced by expensive flats, although the mill leat still runs under the buildings. (*Author*)

An early view of Abingdon Lock from below. The Saxons called Abingdon Scovechesham. It was then renamed Abbendon (town of the abbey) when the abbey was founded in 675. A lock was referred to here in the fourteenth century, almost certainly a flash lock in the proximity of the existing weir. In 1316, men complained that they could not get to Oxford because the abbot had made the 'lokes' too high. (*Author*)

Looking up to Abingdon Lock in 2007 and the severe bank erosion becomes clear compared to the previous view. In Thames Conservancy orders the following handwritten note is found: 'Lock and weir keepers are reminded of the order dated June 1903 under which they are forbidden to kill, injure or trap any otters which may be found in or adjacent to the river.' (*Author*)

Looking downstream to Abingdon Bridge with the Abbey Mill chimney visible to the right and Maud Hales Bridge on the left. Abbey Mill was built by Ethelwold and mentioned in the Domesday Book as paying no dues. By the sixteenth century it was also know as 'Byn milles' and had three water mills and one fulling mill in ruins. In 1583, labourers were paid 12*d* for two days of 'shovelinge gravel' out of the Thames at Abyndun. (*Author*)

Looking downstream at Abingdon in 2007, as close to the original as possible. The erosion here has been reversed with the bank protection giving the river a manufactured look. During the floods of 2007 many boats were caught out and in danger of becoming beached on the bank. Fortunately, a quick-thinking local scaffolding firm erected barriers to prevent this. (*Author*)

Looking downstream from Abingdon Bridge in about 1908 towards the distant wharf and St Helen's church. Already much of the bank on the left has been protected but the island to the right of the view remains lush with vegetation. (*Author*)

The same view from Abingdon Bridge in 2007. The island on the right has changed greatly with the development of a boat hire and chandlery business. The serenity of the previous view has vanished with boats littered in every available mooring space. (*Author*)

2

ABINGDON TO SHIPLAKE

The three mills of Cleeve, Mapledurham and Shiplake have had mixed fortunes over the years. Cleeve has been converted into accommodation, Mapledurham has journeyed from the brink of collapse back to being a working mill and a popular visitor attraction, while Shiplake mill suffered a fire which completely destroyed it.

In about 1808, changes took place at Culham when the lock and cut were constructed, thus ending the monopoly of the mill owner at Sutton Courtenay 'mylle and moates' to charge his exorbitant tolls to pass the mill. The long and tranquil backwater leading up to the former mill site is worth visiting by boat.

Looking upstream towards Abingdon Wharf, probably in the late 1890s. On the far left of the view is the bridge over the entrance to the Wilts & Berks Canal. The canal was not particularly successful and cost £255,000 to build. It was slow in its completion; the last 18 miles to Abingdon Wharf took five years to complete. Unfortunately, the coming of Brunel's railway sounded the death knell for this waterway, despite the use of the canal for transporting railway supplies. (*Author*)

The same view photographed in 2007 shows an astonishing amount of tree growth obscuring the old gaol and most of St Helen's church spire. The entrance bridge to the Wilts and Berks canal has gone and the entrance has been filled in. Only two noticeable features remain from the earlier view: the Old Anchor Inn and the cast iron bridge over the River Ock. (*Author*)

A Henry Taunt view looking upstream towards Culham Lock with the lock cut and footbridge in the background. In 1801 there was a survey undertaken to investigate the possibility of a pound lock and cut at Culham to bypass Sutton Mills which was an expensive and difficult route to navigate. It took a further eight years for this bypass to open. (*Oxfordshire County Council Photographic Archive*)

Culham Lock upstream 2007, photographed from the road bridge. It is quite a contrast from the earlier bleak rural scene, with trees and vegetation softening the lock cut. The current lock house is at least the third on this site, built in 1958. (*Author*)

Built in 1822, Clifton Lock is a relatively new structure although there were earlier suggestions to locate a lock close to Clifton Bridge. The original lock cottage is still visible so this view was taken before 1929 when the cottage was demolished.

In the late 1940s there was an infestation of water voles on the lock island here and the Navigation Inspectorate along with Oxfordshire Agricultural Executive Committee agreed an extermination program using cyanide gas. With numbers in severe decline and often mistaken for water rats, water voles are now a protected species. (*Author*)

Looking downstream to Clifton Lock in 2008. The nearside bank has been protected to provide mooring for the lock, while the opposite bank has an older style of protection. Just visible to the right of the view is the small 'house' weir also referred to as a 'tumbling bay' or 'lasher' weir. (*Author*)

Looking downstream from the tail of Days Lock in the 1920s with the Sinodun Hill Forts in the distance. Like most Thames locks, Days started life as a flash lock and weir, possibly as long ago as 1580. In 1871, the Conservators decreed that lock keepers were forbidden to take in paying lodgers with the exception of this lock, as the house here did not belong to the Conservators. The footbridge was erected in 1870, replacing a former swing bridge and now hosts the International Pooh Sticks Competition, raising much needed funds for the Royal National Lifeboat Institute. (*Author*)

Apart from the trees on the right-hand bank and moorings to the left, little has changed in this view of Days Lock looking downstream in 2007. (*Author*)

A very early view of Days Lock looking upstream with the lock cottage on the left. Thames historian Fred Thacker refers to obstructions in the river below Days Lock; could this be the remnants of the earlier flash weir at this site? It is unusual to find the lock house so far away from the lock itself. (*Steve Capel-Davies*)

With much scrambling and cursing, this was the closest modern photograph that could be obtained in 2007 of Days Lock and Bridge upstream without falling in the river! (*Author*)

Looking down to the bridge at Shillingford from the nearby hill, date unknown. There was a ferry crossing at Shillingford in 1378, yet a bridge was referred to as early as 1301. On the far side of the bridge is the toll cottage and although toll collection ended in 1874, the cottage was not demolished until 1937. Note the osiers stacked by the bridge and the horse grazing nearby. (*David Beasley*)

An approximation of the view from the hill down to Shillingford Bridge taken in 2007, made difficult by the amount of trees and bushes. On the land where the horse once grazed, there is now a riverside swimming pool owned by the nearby Shillingford Bridge Hotel. (*Author*)

Looking upstream to Benson Lock, date unknown. Banesinga, Bynsington, Bensington and eventually becoming Benson, clearly easier to pronounce. There was a mill on the Crowmarsh side of the Thames at Benson in 1396, but a pound lock was not built here until 1788, inevitably following on from the much earlier flash lock and weir. During these early days the miller also ran Benson Lock and weir; this was not a great idea as he was often away tending to his milling business (and probably ensuring there was a sufficient head of water at the weir to turn the mill wheel). (*David Beasley*)

A 2007 view of Benson Lock with resident lock keeper Bob Mainwaring kindly filling the lock helping to approximate the earlier view. It was not possible, of course, to only have one gate open! (*Author*)

Looking upstream to Benson Lock and weir with haphazard piling and shoals clearly visible. Lack of dredging here is nothing new. There have been shoals below this lock for many years and despite numerous vessels running aground, the shoals remain a movable hazard to navigation. It was at this lock in the 1950s that the lock keeper was bribed (sorry, tipped) by a famous boater the princely sum of £5 to keep quiet about his mistress who was installed at the nearby Shillingford Bridge Hotel while his wife was still on board the boat in blissful ignorance. (*David Beasley*)

As close to the earlier view as was possible, below Benson Lock, 2007. The weir is no longer the paddle and rymer version and the cutwater below the lock has been improved for boat moorings. The shoals below the lock mentioned in the previous caption provide the lock staff with a source of entertainment as boats still run aground on a regular basis. (*Author*)

An early view of Percy Turner's boat sheds at lower wharf, Wallingford. Although Mr Turner was primarily a boat builder, he later used the wharf area for swimming and boating. According to the sign above the shed he also bought, sold and repaired boats as well as selling teas. (*Justin Nelson*)

Wallingford lower wharf site, 2007. With only a slight view of one roof line to identify the location, this view was probably one of the most difficult photographs to take. It is worthy of inclusion to demonstrate just how much has changed along the Thames over the years. (*Author*)

Cleeve Lock photographed by Henry Taunt in 1890. Cleeve Lock, originally an open-sided timber lock, was reconstructed as a pound lock in 1787 at a cost of £1,000. The workmen were given beer while they worked and gin if they worked in the water. Whoever thought that was a good idea? (*Oxfordshire County Council Photographic Archive*)

Cleeve Lock photographed on a late November day in 2007. The quaint lock cottage has gone, replaced by the current house in 1958. (*Author*)

Cleeve Mill photographed by Reading photographer Philip Collier, date unknown. The word Cleeve is a derivation from a word meaning either cliff or clift; describing the action of water cutting or making a channel. John Pitman was miller here in 1802 and ran both the mill and the lock. Have a guess where his loyalties lay? The seventeenth-century mill ground corn from 1888 onwards but is now in private hands. (*Museum of English Rural Life*)

Cleeve Mill photographed in 2007 from a slightly different angle to avoid the trees completely obscuring the view. This mill once had two wheels and five millstones. One of the undershot wheels remains to this day. Although it is working, it is unconnected. The grounds in front of the mill have been extended and the wooden building in the previous view is now brick built. Inside the building with the balcony, flood marks for the years 1751, 1799, 1809 and 1947 are scored elegantly into the brickwork. (*Author*)

Goring Lock photographed from the bridge, date unknown. In 1538 there was reference to a house, weir, windmill, priory and ferry at this location. There were problems with shallows here, owing to the millers both here and at Cleeve refusing to release water; only small boats could move as a result. In 1868, a lock house was suggested so that the 'lock keeper had no excuse for being absent from the lock.' (*Author*)

Goring photographed from the bridge in the aftermath of the 2007 floods; evidence of which may be seen on the lower lay-by. The Thames Conservancy stores list of 1905 included one pair of leather water boots and cap, half a ton of coal, two gallons of paraffin oil and one drag line. (*Author*)

Looking downstream to Goring Lock in about 1916. Two ancient tracks, the Ridgeway and the Icknield Way, come down to the river below Goring Lock and there was also the likelihood of a Roman causeway across the river on the line of the bridge. (*Ken Townsend*)

Goring Lock in 2007 shows the lock house has been extended and trees are now obscuring the church and the bridge. (*Author*)

Whitchurch Lock looking downstream towards the toll bridge, date unknown. A flash lock existed at Whitchurch as early as 1580 with the flashes timetabled on Wednesdays at 5.30 a.m. and Saturdays at the more civilised hour of 8.30 a.m. Barges were winched upstream through the weir by the winch on the north bank, aided by two sets of rollers, one in the weir, the other close to the Swan public house. There were two mills here, a corn mill on the north bank and a thimble mill just upstream from the River Pang. (*Environment Agency*)

Despite waiting for some considerable time for it to move, this 2007 view of Whitchurch Lock includes a narrow boat that was moored upstream of the lock. The boat in the foreground is one of many moored on private land above the lock. The 1829 lock cottage seen here is still in use today, albeit modernised and extended and in the background Whitchurch Bridge is just visible. (*Author*)

An early view of Whitchurch Mill taken from below the toll bridge, date unknown. On a 1786 map Whitchurch was marked as a corn mill. In 1866, mills such as Whitchurch were transferred to the Thames Conservancy with compensation paid to the owners, 'so that private interests should no longer interfere with the navigation of one of the most important highways of the kingdom.' *(Philip Emerton)*

A 2009 photograph taken from Whitchurch Bridge Toll House garden. The mill buildings have additions and the riverbank has been protected, otherwise little has changed. The house to the right of the church was once the residence of a Thames fisherman, John Champ, who was noted as in favour of 'brethren of the angle.' *(Author)*

Shooter's Hill looking downstream towards Pangbourne, date unknown. Legend has it that a notorious highwayman could not be pursued from Berkshire into Oxfordshire and he was shot at from the top of this hill. It is probably just a legend, but cannon balls from a Civil War artillery post were discovered when the embankment for the Great Western Railway was raised. (*David Beasley*)

Shooter's Hill photographed from more or less the same vantage point in 2007. What was once a quiet dirt track is now a very busy road with Victorian properties all the way to Pangbourne. The huge embankment, so bare in the earlier view, is covered with mature trees. The river is not sloping down to the right; it is an optical illusion owing to the width of this reach. (*Author*)

The 1894 Thames flood in Pangbourne village, photographed by the Tidbury brothers of Pangbourne. This flood, along with the one in 1947, were two of the worst Thames floods recorded and caused many difficulties including temporary wooden boardwalks and the use of punts to get around, as seen here. This location is quite some distance from the Thames but the River Pang runs nearby, which no doubt contributed to the flooding. (*Hilary Fisher*)

This view of Pangbourne in 2007 took a great deal of time to take as this junction is extremely busy. Most of the buildings on the left of the view remain more or less the same as they were in 1894. Mortimore's the former grocer, provision merchant and tobacconist's shop has had windows added and is now Lane Fox Estate Agents. (*Author*)

Mapledurham Lock from below, date unknown. At one time called Mawple Durham, there was a weir attached to the nearby mill from 1270. For a meagre 24 shillings a month in 1854, the lock keeper had to look after the lock as well as the two ferries at Roebuck and Purley. The pound lock opened in 1777, was rebuilt in 1867, restored in 1888 and had a completely new lock built alongside the old one in 1907/8. This proves the theory that poor quality building and materials will always require remedial work. In 1853, the lock keeper had his wages halved but was allowed to keep the income from pleasure tolls. (*Environment Agency*)

Mapledurham Lock photographed in 2007. A huge amount of bank protection work has occurred here as well as some weir improvements, although the weir still has paddle and rymers in part. What was probably the old lock house in the previous view has gone and the current house was built in 1931 on the opposite bank. (*Author*)

Above Mapledurham Mill, date unknown. Within the structure of this mill some of the fifteenth-century timbers and roof trusses are still visible. Part of the entry for this mill in the Domesday Book reads 'William de Warene holds Malpederham of the King... There is a mill worth 20 shillings and 10 acres of meadow. It was worth in the time of King Edward and afterwards 8 pounds, now 12 pounds.' (*David Beasley*)

A similar view of the mill taken in 2007. The 1777 storage barn (on the right in the previous view) has gone and there are now plastic chairs on the grass instead of logs. This mill is grinding wholemeal flour once more and has regular open days when one can follow the milling operation from start to finish. (*Author*)

Mapledurham Mill from below photographed by H.S. Adams in about 1904. Millers at Mapledurham were recorded in the Court Rolls of 1437, 1444 and 1445 when they were summoned by the Court. Around 1670, a second wheel was added; this drove two more pairs of mill stones, making four in total. (*Hilary Fisher*)

Mapledurham Mill taken in 2007, admittedly from not quite the same angle as the earlier view. Despite asking permission to photograph the mill, this was overruled by another party and I was invited to leave, hence the slightly wrong angle! (*Author*)

A busy scene looking upstream from Caversham Bridge, date unknown. Numerous boats for hire, a waterside petrol pump and distant chimneys complete the scene. To the right of the view is Reading Engineering Works who were engineers, iron and brass founders. (*Author*)

The view from Caversham Bridge in 2007 bears no resemblance to the previous image. In fact, it was very difficult to decide where to take this photograph from as there were no landmarks or features to compare it to. (*Author*)

Photographed in about 1867, this view shows Caversham Bridge in two halves. There was a chapel situated here and money for the upkeep of the bridge was donated by pilgrims traveling to visit religious relics, the authenticity of which were exaggerated. The long-running dispute between the County of Oxfordshire and the Corporation of Reading was finally resolved and a continuous iron bridge costing £10,000 was opened in July 1869. Visible on the far bank is Cawston's white house from which boats were 'let on hire at moderate charges.' (*Philip Emerton*)

...rsham Bridge from more or less the same angle as the previous view. The central pier in this ... was the site of St Anne's chapel. Stonework footings of this chapel were discovered during ...onstruction of this new bridge which finally opened in 1926. (*Author*)

Marked on the postcard as Thames Bank and probably photographed before 1907, this photograph taken at Reading shows W. Moss's boat building premises on the right where boats were also 'let or housed'. The barge *Swallow* is just visible in front of a loading crane; to the left of the chimney is probably Allen's yard and making its way upstream is the Thames Conservancy tug *Cherwell*. (*Graham Parlour*)

Reading has probably undergone the most changes of a Thames-side town. Here in 2007 is the view of the end of Thames Avenue. All the buildings in the previous view have gone, replaced with houses and apartments. There is a ferry service over to Fry's Island on the left of the view for the wonderfully named 'Island Bohemian Bowls Club'. Fry's Island was once known as De Montfort Island after Robert de Montfort who inflicted serious injury on Henry of Essex in 1163 who was undergoing 'trial by combat' for cowardice and treachery. (*Author*)

Sonning Lock and keeper, date unknown. In a survey of the Thames in 1578 there were 23 locks, 16 mills, 16 floodgates and 7 wears (weirs) between Maidenhead and Oxford. Two years later another manuscript refers to 'An old ruinous weare in the pish (parish) of Suning.' Before work on Sonning Lock commenced the towing path between the lock and Sonning Bridge was constructed at a cost of £2 8s. The labourers earned 1s 6d daily; carpenters were paid more at 2s per day. All workers were given beer to drink. Water was unsafe to drink in those times and 'small beer' was the safer alternative. The phrase 'small beer' comes from the practice of brewing a second batch of beer from the same mash, creating a weaker drink. (*Ken Townsend*)

Sonning Lock in 2007, the house in the previous view was replaced in 1916. Just below the lock, tucked out of sight, is a memorial gate to Denys Amos, master of Reading Blue Coat School who drowned near here on 26 January 1953. (*Author*)

It is possible that John Treacher, who constructed the towpath at Sonning, may have built this fine and much photographed bridge at Sonning. Early river bridges were often made of cheap timber and did not last very long. Rumours of a wooden Saxon crossing here in 1125 persist but no definite evidence can be found. In the background of this photograph is the White Hart, which dates back to Elizabethan times, and in the foreground is a thriving boat hire business. (*Author*)

Once again, it was not possible to take this 2007 photo of Sonning Bridge from exactly the same place as the previous view for fear of falling in. The only remnants of the boat hire business is a mooring post and scattered lumps of concrete. The 1729 brick built bridge has suffered from the huge volume of traffic and has been reinforced recently in addition to a traffic light-controlled one-way system. (*Author*)

A romantic ivy-clad Shiplake Lock captured by Reading photographer Philip Collier from the site of the old mill whose foundation stones may be seen in the foreground. The pound lock here was built in 1773 out of fir which failed to last and was substituted eventually with oak; it was rebuilt once more in 1874 from stone. (*Philip Emerton*)

A closer view of Shiplake Lock complete with steam launch in 2007. There is a tall hedge in front of the old mill foundation stones preventing exactly the same view being taken. The mill here had two sluices and the channels may still be seen, although the walls have gone completely. (*Author*)

Shiplake Mill from below the lock, date unknown. Shiplake Mill initially ground corn and then became a paper mill. Possibly dating back as early as 1404 and referred to as Cotterell's, it caught fire and was demolished in 1907. (*Hilary Fisher*)

Astonishing that this flimsy boat shed is still here after all these years, despite the demolition of the mill. Is it the same one? The site of the mill has been obscured by trees and there is little to see on this potentially dangerous site which is full of hidden holes and fallen masonry. Below the lock from where this view was taken was once a series of small islands, known locally as 'the crocodile'. These were joined together to form the lock moorings we see today. (*Author*)

3

SHIPLAKE TO BOVENEY LOCK

The mills that once stood on the banks have disappeared completely apart from Hambledon which has somehow survived. There are no traces whatsoever of Hurley Mill. Temple Mills, which operated for at least 300 hundred years, have been demolished and replaced with luxury riverside properties. Marlow Mills have suffered the same fate. The uneconomic ferry crossings have ceased to operate; only the name remains here and there on a house or lane. The popular lock at Boulter's still attracts onlookers on a sunny day, but nowhere near the amount it did on Ascot Sunday in the 1920s.

A downstream view to Marsh Lock, date unknown. There was a flash lock at Marsh dating from 1580; in 1746 it was known as 'mash' lock. A pound lock was constructed here in 1773 and rebuilt in 1787. (*Philip Emerton*)

The lock house of 1813 at Marsh remains the same in this 2007 view as well as the large white house. The right-hand bank has considerable growth hiding the buildings and, as with most locks, walkways for lock moorings have been installed. (*Author*)

Looking upstream towards Marsh Mills, here we see the Horse Bridge and distant lock in 1879. There were two distinctly separate mills at Marsh, the two mills on the Berkshire bank ground corn while the mills on the Oxfordshire side ground corn and produced paper, at least until 1893. (*Philip Emerton*)

Marsh Mills and the distant lock in 2008 present a different outlook. The Berkshire mills were in part pulled down in about 1970 and there are now apartments with river views available to rent. The Oxfordshire mills that were once known as New Mills are no longer there as usage ceased in the early twentieth century. (*Author*)

Looking downstream to Henley Bridge photographed by Henry Taunt in about 1890. Taunt was a prolific Thames photographer. His patience and skill at composition are shown in this deserted view of Henley, probably taken early in the day. (*Author*)

A very different view downstream of Henley Bridge, taken in 2007. The grassy bank has given way to concrete sandbags and mooring piles, while the section from the bridge upstream is no longer the uncluttered scene from the previous view. (*Author*)

An image of Hambledon Lock taken from a Victorian lantern slide, date unknown. In 1376 this small village was called Hamelden and there was evidence of a single-gated flash lock here dating from the fourteenth century. It didn't acquire its pound lock until 1773. A year later the lock keeper had a small wooden house built for him at a cost of £12. During the Second World War, enemy aircraft dropped bombs in a nearby field. The blast was so fierce that lock keeper Thomas Wise was blown off the weir and shrapnel punched a hole through the oak door of the house. Even during the 1960s there was no electricity, mains water or flush toilets at this lock. (*Author*)

The bank erosion seen in the previous view of Hambledon has been remedied with mooring for the lock. The entire lock was rebuilt and widened in 1993/4 with the addition of a unique under-floor filling system. The traditional sluices were relocated to the bullnose chambers where they were linked into the lock chamber by four 82 centimetre diameter pipes. These huge pipes were in turn linked to thirty-six 300 millimetre diameter nozzles. This giant Jacuzzi can move an amazing 679,000 litres of water in or out of the lock safely in three and a half minutes with a great deal less turbulence. (*Author*)

Hambledon Mill photographed in about 1890. Probably one of the most photographed Thames mills, Hambledon gets a mention in the Domesday Book of 1086, but it had stopped working by 1952. There was never a mill wheel here, only a turbine which supplied electricity for the village. (*Author*)

Hambledon Mill photographed from the weir walkway in 2007. The houses and buildings in the area around the mill were all named after the owners of the buildings. The mill still has its sluice gates as well as the turbine, albeit disconnected. With interest in renewable energy sources, perhaps some Thames mills such as Hambledon could be converted to generate electricity? (*Author*)

A Henry Taunt view of Medmenham Hotel and ferry, probably with the ferryman and boat in the foreground, date unknown. In 1873 Medmenham Hotel was managed by H.J. Todd and *The Globe* described it as 'The snuggest Inn on the river.' It was also 'replete with every comfort [for] pleasure boats, punts and fishing men'. (*Author*)

A 2007 view of the Medmenham Hotel and ferry site, neither of which exist today. The ferry was once operated by the hotel and a dispute arose whether the ferry was public. The hotelier charged an excessive toll to cross and it is possible that this instigated two court actions to determine whether or not there were ancient ferry rights here. Hudson Kearley, the first Viscount Davenport, won the case in the Appeal Court in 1899 and erected a grand monument to that fact. A pyrrhic victory however – the ferry ceased operation after the Second World War. (*Author*)

Hurley Lock bathing place below the weir, photographed in the 1930s. Difficult to believe today, but swimming in the River Thames was a popular pastime actively encouraged by the Thames Conservancy. Steps, diving board, changing tents and a lifeguard hut all feature in this busy view. (*Ken Townsend*)

The old bathing place at Hurley looks forlorn compared to the earlier view. The huts on the right are public toilets and waste disposal for boaters. As far as could be discovered, swimming continued here until at least 1956. Marked on a Thames Conservancy survey map of that date were the changing rooms, lifeguard hut and Elsan toilets. (*Author*)

An 1894 Victorian lantern slide view looking downstream to Hurley Lock complete with houseboat. Houseboats were in abundance in Victorian times, many being towed to Henley for the regatta. Houseboats were for the very wealthy. One such vessel was advertised for sale around this time at £450. Failing that, for £50 one could rent one for three days already moored at Henley. (*Author*)

A view taken over one hundred years later and many changes have taken place. The elegant houseboat from the previous view has been replaced with cruisers, sometimes unkindly referred to by lock keepers as gin palaces or plastic boats. (*Author*)

This photograph of Hurley Lock taken in 1903 demonstrates the popular misconception of the idyllic life of a Thames lock keeper: cows grazing, a few visitors and the lock keeper idly sitting on the lock beam waiting for boats. There was once a mill on the island which burnt down in 1887. It was quickly rebuilt and was operating once more two years later. (*Author*)

The right-hand wing wall of the lock appears to be the only part that hasn't changed compared to the 1903 lantern slide view. The old lock house has gone, demolished and a new house built on the left-hand bank in 1959. The towpath changes banks twice here, bridge crossings provided above and below the lock. The upstream bridge was once named 'silly bridge' although it is unclear why. (*Author*)

Certainly photographed before 1932 when it was demolished after a fire, Temple House epitomised all that was elegant on the banks of the Thames at that time. Designed by architect Samuel Wyatt and owned by Temple Mill owner Thomas Williams, the interior was said to be spectacular. According to Mrs Powys in 1796, the interior featured 'statues of every kind, an aviary full of all kinds of birds, flying loose in a large octagon of gilt wire,' as well as a 'fountain illuminated by wax lights, where the water falls down some rockwork in the form of a cascade.' (*Ray Evans*)

A similar view of the same stretch of river above Temple Lock, photographed in 2007. It is possible that the 'Danger' board is made of the same stuff as the Thames Conservancy used for most of their piling work due to its longevity, the tropical hardwood Greenheart. A great shame that the elegant Temple House was not rebuilt after the fire as the aspect today does nothing to enhance the view. (*Author*)

In this view taken in about 1917, two launches leave Temple Lock watched by the ever-present spectators. The word Temple denotes an ancient connection to the Knights Templar and this guild of men were given a great deal of land throughout England. In return for these gifts, they protected pilgrims on their way to Jerusalem. (*Author*)

Temple Lock looking downstream with Temple Mill houses just visible in the background. The present lock was built alongside the original 1790 lock which was converted into boat rollers; the old lock cottage was demolished in 1958. A ferry operated above the lock until 1953 and the old ferry hut is still on the lock island. A much higher towpath bridge replaced the original bridge in 1989 providing the walker with lovely views. (*Author*)

An 1889 Victorian lantern slide view of Temple Weir Pool with Temple Lock in the distance. Photographed from Temple Mill Island, a site once owned by the Knights Templar who also held the estate at nearby Bisham. (*Author*)

A 2007 view taken from Mill Island shows little has changed; the weir was completely rebuilt in 1975 which included a fish ladder but the older overflow can still be seen underwater. (*Author*)

Looking downstream towards Marlow Bridge and All Saints' church, date unknown. In 1227, Henry III made a gift of oak to repair the earlier bridge situated at the end of St Peter's Street further downstream. Subsequent bridges collapsed or fell into the river. Finally Tierney Clark's elegant suspension bridge, seen here, opened in 1832. Even this bridge had problems in 1927 when the decking had to be replaced and weight restrictions imposed. It is now a Grade I structure of historical importance. (*Unknown*)

Taken from Rivermead Court in 2007, All Saints' church and Marlow Suspension Bridge are the only two features that have remained unchanged from the previous view. The riverside flats to the left of the bridge were built in 1972 and named Tierney Court after the bridge builder. Boats no longer anchor in mid-stream and the river appears much wider, probably owing to housing developments and bank protection. (*Author*)

The Compleat Angler upstream of Marlow Weir, date unknown. This was originally a pub called the Riverside Inn and owned by Wethered Brewery. This popular riverside destination changed its name soon after the publication of Izaak Walton's fishing book *The Compleat Angler* was published in 1653. With its wonderful views and staff discretion it has always been popular with celebrities from different eras such as J.M.Barrie, Scott Fitzgerald, Noel Coward and Nancy Mitford, and in more recent times Omar Sharif, Clint Eastwood, Naomi Campbell and the late Princess Diana. In June 1999, Her Majesty the Queen dined here privately at the invitation of the President of Hungary, Arpad Goncz. (*Environment Agency*)

A modern view of The Compleat Angler taken from the grounds of All Saints' churchyard in 2007. Not exactly the same angle as a high wall proved a restriction. Considerably extended and improved over many years, this riverside hotel bears little resemblance to the previous view, apart from the main building. (*Author*)

A view across the Thames to the end of St Peter's Street taken from Marlow Weir, date unknown. Now a public slipway, this street led to the former bridge across the river. There was a capstan situated here in 1753, enabling vessels to be winched up through the 'old ware'. There were also two wharves, Poor's Wharf here and another one closer to the lock on the same bank. There were at least two pubs as well to service the nearby wharves, the Two Brewers, which is still there, and the now-vanished Fisherman's Retreat. (*Marlow Society*)

Across the river to St Peter's Street in 2007, this looks nothing like the earlier view and it was difficult to determine the correct angle with no reference points. Old Bridge House on the left of the view was built sometime after 1872 when all the old cottages to the left of the slipway were demolished. (*Author*)

A close-up of the main weir at Marlow, nicknamed the 'Lion's Mouth' probably owing to the roar of the water passing through. These sluices show how difficult and dangerous it must have been to operate these early weirs, never mind having to winch your barge upstream through them! Just visible behind the bridge on the right is the huge barn belonging to Bisham Abbey. It was demolished in 1878 and was previously used as a coal store and gaol for French prisoners during the war. After demolition, some of its beams ended up in a church roof in nearby Lane End. (*Environment Agency*)

Impossible to duplicate the previous view but the Thames still roars through the two main bucks in the centre of this 2007 photograph. The weed-infested overflow has been completely transformed into one of the most attractive and photogenic scenes on the River Thames. (*Author*)

Looking towards Marlow Lock in about 1915 from the corner of Mill Road. Prior to a pound lock being built here in 1773, vessels were winched through the old weir; this type of weir is sometimes referred to as a flash lock. Flashes wasted huge amounts of water and the river here was often left dry for twenty-four hours after a flash. (*Author*)

Expensive boats waiting to pass through Marlow Lock photographed in 2008. The old lock cottage has gone, replaced in 1959 with the present house. The mill buildings seen to the left of the earlier view were demolished in 1965, replaced with weatherboarded houses. (*Author*)

A close-up view of the mills at Marlow taken from the footbridge that leads to the lock. In 1939, the entire site could be bought for only £2,000. When the modern mill houses were up for sale in about 1965 they were priced between £16,000 and £18,000. One of these houses recently went on the market at £1.2 million. (*Unknown*)

The same view of the mill site taken in 2008 from the footbridge. Nothing remains of the old mill buildings in the previous view, however there is a sluice on the left to manage the flow of water. It is almost certain that the boat house to the right is the same one as in the previous view, judging by the decorative tiles at the edge of the roof. (*Author*)

Looking upstream towards Marlow Lock and Mills, date unknown. A mill was mentioned here in the Domesday Book of 1086 and there were three mills here in 1753: New Mill, Corn Mill and Oil Mill. In 1816, these processes gave way to the production of paper. (*Ken Townsend*)

Looking towards Marlow Mills, photographed in 2007. The lock island on the left of the view has been divided up into smaller and smaller building plots over the years and a number of the temporary buildings are now permanently occupied for which the residents pay the Environment Agency a 'toll' to cross the lock gates. To capture this view, it was necessary to be perched precariously over the river. (*Author*)

A Victorian lantern slide view looking upstream from Bourne End railway bridge towards Townsend's Boatyard, 1905. The former Hurley lock keeper, Robert Townsend, bought one of the derelict wharves here and started building skiffs, dinghies, punts and canoes as well as the steamer *Vigilant*. During both world wars Townsend's Boatyard built lifeboats for the Royal Navy. (*Author*)

Looking upstream from Bourne End railway bridge in 2007 and only the round house to the right of the view remains the same. Townsend's Boatyard has gone following the decline in river traffic and was sold off to establish a marina in the 1960s. (*Author*)

A Henry Taunt postcard view taken in 1875 from the tower of Holy Trinity Church looking down on Cookham Bridge. To the left of the view edged with trees is Hedsor Water, the former navigation channel until 1830 when it was bypassed with a lock cut. (*Hilary Fisher*)

It took some time to arrange permission to take this photograph from the top of Holy Trinity Church in Cookham and on the day the weather was slightly hazy. The trees have grown and only a small part of the meadow is visible and none of the lock cut or Hedsor Water may be seen. The large building on the riverbank is D.B. Marine. (*Author*)

Looking towards the Ferry Inn at Cookham, date unknown. Like most Thames bridges, Cookham replaced an earlier ferry and before work could begin on the bridge, the ferry rights had to be bought at a cost of £2,275. This bridge was a toll bridge and these tolls continued until 1947, when it was made free at a cost of £30,000. The toll collector's cottage just survived demolition and has been painstakingly restored in recent years. (*Author*)

The lane leading down to the former ferry is still there but little else remains the same in this 2007 view of The Ferry. On the wall inside this recently refurbished gastro pub is a fine image of the old ferry in operation. Moored outside are a narrowboat and a former River Thames Police launch, aptly named *Old Billy*. (*Author*)

A Victorian lantern slide view of Cookham Lock, date unknown. Navigation through the many channels in this area had been difficult with rock falls, shallows and sunken vessels in Hedsor Water not helping matters. The 1830 cut and lock bypassed Hedsor Water and robbed wharf owner Lord Boston of his tolls and by stealth, Hedsor Water became cut off to navigation. A Public Right of Navigation has existed for hundreds of years on the River Thames and in a complex and protracted legal case brought by Josie Rowland against the Environment Agency, this Public Right of Navigation was challenged. Her lawsuit eventually failed in this assertion and Hedsor Water can no longer be regarded as 'private' because a Public Right of Navigation exists on all waters connected to the Thames according to the law. For an interesting and lengthy read, have a look at the following internet link: www.4-graysinnsquare.co.uk/cases (*Author*)

Cookham Lock from about the same place in 2007. This location has had a great deal of bank protection and moorings added, although it still remains one of the most pleasant Thames locks to visit with Hedsor Woods towering over the whole area. (*Author*)

Cookham Lock Cottage with elegant visitors photographed in 1902. Above the door of the cottage is a board displaying the lock keeper's name, Alfred Hill. Like many lock keepers at that time, he sold refreshments to the public and boaters alike; in this case Schweppes lemonade. (*Author*)

Extended and greatly improved, the Cookham Lock Cottage of 1902 can still be seen as part of the current house. The resident lock keeper assures me that he will not be selling Schweppes lemonade! (*Author*)

Looking downstream to Boulter's Lock in about 1908. This pound lock was constructed in 1772 and the name is probably derived from bolting, a milling term for sieving. The mill on Ray Mill Island to the left of the view was noted in 1348 as 'Reye Mulles' and the name Ray appears on many nearby roads. Ray Mill Island was owned by the Ray family until it was eventually bought by Sir Thomas Bodley in 1608. Monies from the mills here funded part of the Bodleian Library at Oxford. (*Author*)

Boulter's Lock in 2007 with an altogether wider approach to the lock, as well as very different craft. The first building on the left has gone and there is a different bridge at the tail of the lock. There are currently apartments being built by Hadley Homes on part of the island (going the way of many a mill site) where Richard Dimbleby CBE once lived. (*Author*)

Photographed in about 1902, Boulter's Lock is packed with small boats of every description. A favoured destination on Ascot Sunday, the place to see and be seen for high society. (*Author*)

A much quieter day at Boulter's Lock in 2007. River traffic has gone into decline in recent years as mentioned elsewhere and a recent announcement has been made by the Environment Agency proposing lock keeper redundancies. Will the Thames locks ever become completely self-service? There is already public power available at selected locks and one cannot help wondering about the legal implications of the lock keepers' absence in the event of an accident. (*Author*)

Looking towards Ray Mill Island with the impressive Glen Island House on the right. Now Grade II listed, Glen Island House was built in 1869 for Lieutenant-General Sir Roger Palmer. Something of a steam boat enthusiast, he was one of the survivors of the Charge of the Light Brigade during the Crimean War. (*Author*)

A fine example of tree growth with Glen Island House now completely surrounded by trees. The bank on the left has changed somewhat with bank protection and a tree-lined promenade from Maidenhead Bridge to Boulter's Lock. (*Author*)

Looking upstream towards Maidenhead Bridge with Bridge Eyot to the left. It would appear that there were several small boat firms letting out the elegant boats seen in this view. *(Unknown)*

The same view in 2007 shows that the small trees on Bridge Eyot have matured and the boat hire has given way to moorings. The distant boathouses in the previous view have been replaced with apartments. *(Author)*

Looking down on Skindles Hotel from Maidenhead Bridge, date unknown. There was an inn here as early as 1743 when John Marsh leased the land from the council for 20s a year. There was another name change to the Orkney Arms in 1833 when it was bought by former waiter William Skindle. In the 1920s and '30s Skindles was the preferred destination for adulterers as it was a quick train ride away from London and the area rapidly became known as Soho-on-Thames. Many rock bands played Skindles in the 1970s including Judas Priest, Curved Air, the Stranglers Thin Lizzy, AC/DC and the Rolling Stones. John Lennon, Yoko Ono and Eric Clapton were present at a gig the Stones played in 1971 before leaving for France. Mick Jagger was so incensed that the sound was switched off at two in the morning, he threw a table through a plate-glass window! (*Author*)

The derelict Skindles Hotel in photographed in 2007 from Maidenhead Bridge. Watchworld developers bought the huge site in 2007 that included Skindles for £30.25 million and sold it on not long after. As this is written, the future of the site is uncertain but the current owners are seeking permission for riverside office blocks. (*Author*)

Looking upstream to Maidenhead Bridge, date unknown. Maidenhead is thought to derive its name from a combination of Mai Dun (Taplow hill) and Hythe (Wharf), however there are many other versions relating to the origins of the name. The bridge was reported in 1297 to be 'almost broke down' as many early wooden bridges did. This fine Grade I listed bridge was built in 1777 and remained a toll bridge until 1903 when the gates were dumped in the river by anarchic motorists! (*Environment Agency*)

A 2007 photograph of Maidenhead Bridge taken from the grounds of Maidenhead Rowing Club with the Thames Riviera Hotel on the left. A certain Maidenhead councillor has recently suggested that the Grade I listed bridge should be demolished and replaced with a four-lane stainless steel structure! (*Author*)

Looking upstream to Boveney Lock, date unknown. According to Thames historian Fred Thacker, there was a fishery at Boveney in 1201 and a reference to 'loke' in 1375 after an unpaid toll. In 1255, Boveney was referred to as Abovenhythe, possibly a reference to the wharf here (hythe meaning wharf in Old English). Other sources claim that Boveney means 'above island'. In 1898, the lock keeper here was sacked for selling home-made wine. (*Steve Capel-Davies*)

Some bank protection, landscaping and the mechanisation of the lock appear to be the only changes from the earlier view, apart from the avenue of horse chestnut trees leading down to the lock. Just upstream from the lock is St Mary Magdalene church which once served the spiritual needs of bargees and river men from the nearby wharf. The church is now maintained by the wonderfully named Friends of Friendless Churches. (*Author*)

4

BOVENEY LOCK TO STRAND ON THE GREEN

The Thames Conservancy undertook huge projects to improve navigation, the largest of which was the construction of the Desborough Channel between Shepperton Lock and Walton Bridge which opened in 1935.

Other projects were undertaken including the building of a new lock at Sunbury in 1926, widening and deepening the river at Shepperton and Wheatley's Ait and the rebuilding of the weirs at Molesey and Teddington. There were further improvements at Hampton Court when the bridge was replaced in 1934, including widening, dredging and bank reprofiling.

A much photographed view of Windsor Castle taken from the Brocas Meadows, date unknown. These meadows were named after Sir Bernard Brocas who fought alongside King Edward III at Crecy. For this service he was gifted rights to land around Windsor including a meadow called Etonmede which was later renamed Brocas. There was a regular ferry service running from here to the town and the gentleman with the pole in this view could well be a ferryman. (*Author*)

Windsor Castle taken from the Brocas in 2007 is more or less the same although erosion has played its part in reducing the banks here and trees have grown. There are some remnants of the old landing stages still to be found underneath the trees on this bank. It is possible that Windsor derives its name from winding shore; the Thames certainly meanders in this area. (*Author*)

Looking downstream to Town Bridge with Parkins Boat Builders and the Bridge House Hotel, date unknown. A bridge is thought to have existed here as early as 1100 but the early records give a date of 1172 when tolls were mentioned in accounts. A legal battle erupted in 1897 over the right to charge tolls to cross this bridge. Joseph Taylor challenged these rights (and the Corporation) by firstly refusing to pay and latterly paying the toll witnessed by two policemen. He then issued a writ for the recovery of an unlawful toll and against the barring of the bridge. Taylor lost the first case in May, appealed and won costs in November 1897. The Corporation took the matter to the House of Lords in November 1898 where Taylor won a favourable judgment. A month later, the toll gates were gone, a victory for the individual! (*Justin Nelson*)

Only the bridge remains the same in this view and even the navigation directions have been removed. Windsor Bridge Court flats have replaced the Bridge House Hotel and Parkins has been replaced by a rowing club. (*Author*)

A busy day at Romney Lock, probably in the late 1890s. There were references to a flash lock here known as Bullokeslok which was partly used as a fishery. A pound lock was suggested above Windsor Bridge close to Firework Ait, but was abandoned after local opposition. Romney Lock was finally opened in 1797 but unusually, it had no weir. (*Author*)

Approximately the same view looking downstream to Romney Lock in 2007 with the 1892 Victorian waterworks visible on the right-hand bank. (*Author*)

Looking downstream to Old Windsor Lock, possibly taken in the 1920s judging by the elegantly dressed boaters. Discussions for a lock here took place as early as 1770 but agreement could not be reached with the landowners. The relatively new lock was built in 1822 at a cost of £2,476 and rebuilt in 1889. The entire lock was completely rebuilt again in 1953/4. (*Author*)

Old Windsor Lock photographed in early 2008 during the re-sheeting of the top gates. There was an ancient fishery owned by the Crown on the site of the current weir at Old Windsor referred to as Horned-ore in 1495 when it was gifted to Eton College who held the title for 200 years. It was latterly known as 'New Lock' and replaced with a weir in 1836. (*Author*)

A rare view upstream towards the well known riverside public house, the Bells of Ousley, date unknown. Legend has it that monks from Oxford were transporting the bells of Osney Abbey by barge and agents of Henry VIII were in hot pursuit. Supposedly the barge ran aground near here and the bells were hidden in the oozing mud. The oozing bells or the bells of Ousley? Could this be the origin of the unusual name? (*Unknown*)

A 2008 view looking towards the distant Bells of Ousley. Hardly recognisable from the previous view with lots of bank protection. (*Author*)

Bell Weir Lock was probably named after the first lock keeper of 1817, Charlie Bell. A popular place to visit for locals judging by the amount of people in this view and certainly taken before 1911 when the Anglers Rest inn, seen in the background, was destroyed by fire. (*Unknown*)

Bell Weir in 2007 still has an unprotected bank but is not frequented by people lounging around. The Anglers Rest from the previous view is now the Runnymede Hotel. (*Author*)

Penton Hook Lock seen here is situated in a huge loop (the hook) of the Thames and was constructed in 1814–15. One of the so called City locks of this time, Penton Hook was the furthest upstream. The lock house, although altered and modernised, retains its original shape and the city crest on the façade. In the 1920s, lock keeper Steve Kirby kept rabbits, chickens, ducks and a goat; in the garden were fruit trees and a huge vegetable patch. (*Author*)

A quiet day at Penton Hook Lock shows few alterations from the earlier view. Sensibly the steps on the right have been offset and all the old-style rubbing piles have gone. The lock office has been updated and a much wider lockside walkway has been created. (*Author*)

There was a proposal to build a lock at Chertsey as early as 1793 but as usual with these proposals, nothing came of it until 1813 when this lock was built. Like Goring and Cookham locks, it had an extra set of gates to conserve water, although these were rarely used. (*Environment Agency*)

An uncluttered Chertsey Lock in 2007. The extra lock gates have been removed and the lockside walkways have been extended. In the background on the right is the telemetry mast for broadcasting water levels to the control room in Frimley. (*Author*)

In 1926 the Thames Conservancy decided to photograph all their lock keepers and ferrymen as well as every lock; an exercise that was never repeated. This photograph of the Chertsey Lock keeper Mr H. Arlett is from that collection. It must have been taken around Regatta time judging by the warning notices. (*Environment Agency*)

The Chertsey Lock keeper John Williams photographed in 2008. Compared to the 1926 photograph there have been many changes. There has been a shift towards informality as lock keepers no longer wear the old Navy-style uniform seen in the previous view. Many staff also wear life jackets while on lock duty, essential when working on the weirs. (*Author*)

An early view of Chertsey Bridge photographed from Dumsey Meadow by Alfred Seeley of Richmond Hill. The hotel in the distance advertises billiards and 'landing place' has been painted on the bridge. In 1824, two men were convicted of stealing live swans from Dumsey Meadow and selling them at Leadenhall Market in London. Unfortunately for them, one of the stolen swans only had one eye and was easily identified. They were both sentenced to seven years' transportation. (*Author*)

Little has altered in this 2007 view of Chertsey Bridge taken from Dumsey Meadow. This meadow has been designated as a Site of Special Scientific Interest which so far has saved it from destruction. However, a recent geological survey of the area has identified this meadow as having vast reserves of gravel below it; how much longer can it withstand destruction? (*Author*)

Shepperton Lock photographed before 1925. There were references to a fish weir near here as early as 1086 yet the lock was referred to as a weir as early as 1293. In times of flood, the river would take the easiest route along a section of Thames known as Stoner's Gut or Stone's Gut, possibly named after a local landowner. It was in this breach that the present lock was constructed and opened in 1813. In the background is D'Oyly Carte Island named after Richard D'Oyly, who produced Gilbert and Sullivan operas. (*Author*)

Shepperton Lock in 2007 with resident lock keeper Steve Newman patrolling his domain. The old lock office has been demolished and moved across the lock. Zachary Allnut, secretary to the Thames Commissioners noted in 1805, 'The navigation upwards is attended at times with great difficulty, delay, expense and danger.' (*Author*)

A photograph across the meadows along the proposed line of the Desborough Cut taken near Shepperton in the early 1930s. In 1926, the *Illustrated London News* contained a report and drawings of a series of artificial cuts proposed by the Thames Conservancy Engineers. There were seventeen cuts and relief channels proposed in total, mostly across bends like at Halliford. At the time the estimated cost for the whole scheme was £9 million. The recent Jubilee River (an artificial cut) from Boulter's weir to Black Potts Viaduct cost the Environment Agency £110 million. (*Environment Agency*)

Desborough Cut in 2007. When this image was taken, the noise from flocks of green parakeets filled the air along the cut. Several theories as to how they arrived here include: escapees from Shepperton Studios, an aviary fire where the owner released the birds from certain death, escapees from freight at Heathrow airport and that Jimi Hendrix had something to do with it. The first breeding pair was recorded in the UK in 1855. The population today is estimated at 30,000. (*Author*)

The lower of the two bridges across the Desborough Cut nearing completion, photographed in the early 1930s. According to a plaque on the bridge, 'The work was commenced in 1930 and carried out at the joint expense of H.M. Government, the County Councils of Middlesex and Surrey, and the Conservators.' (*Environment Agency*)

The same view of the cut in 2007 and time has softened the bridge abutments. The old channel leads off to the right around the meandering Halliford bends while the cut forges straight ahead. There are some little known (and underused) Environment Agency moorings just to the right of this bridge. (*Author*)

A 1937 view of Thames Meadow looking downstream to a distant Walton Bridge and Mount Felix on the right. As this meadow would have been liable to flooding it seemed unlikely that it would ever become occupied and there are a few wooden huts and a bus just visible. (*Environment Agency*)

With little in the way of a reference point, this 2007 image of Thames Meadow was difficult to take and demonstrates just how much has changed in this area. The bank has been substantially raised and the numerous residences now completely block the view of Walton Bridge and Mount Felix. (*Author*)

Walton Bridge looking downstream, date unknown. Walton has had its fair share of bridges commencing with the first one in about 1750, replacing a ferry that had ran from the fifteenth century onwards. The bridge seen in this view is the 1864 lattice girder bridge. (*Author*)

A 2007 view of the 1999 'temporary' Walton Bridge. Proposals are being developed to alleviate congestion and access issues. The Environment Agency has insisted that any new bridge scheme has to have the navigation headroom increased and that there are no river piers to impede navigation. This £15 million scheme has recently been abandoned; perhaps one day poor Walton will have a noteworthy river crossing! (*Author*)

This photograph of the backwater at Walton-on-Thames was taken from the parapet of the old bridge looking towards the back of Rosewell's Boatyard, date unknown. The piece of water seen here is known as Walton Sea (sometimes called Walton Sale). The low-lying marshes at the Cowey Sale public space flood in high water and were almost certainly part of the original course of the Thames. Walton Sea and the nearby Broadwater Lake are both reminders of that earlier course. (*Author*)

The former small boatyard at Rosewell's has enlarged and expanded over the years as this 2007 view shows Walton Sea complete with numerous moorings. (*Author*)

An early view upstream to Walton Bridge, date unknown. There is no Rosewell's Boathouse and Walton Sea is huge. The towing path bridge in the foreground was built in about 1805. Visible in the background is the approach causeway to the 1788 brick and stone bridge; to the right is the 1864 lattice girder bridge. (*Environment Agency*)

Inside the boatyard at Walton Marina, 2007. This was one of the most problematic views to photograph owing to a lack of reference points and the marina's wooden fence. The towpath bridge on the right has had a height increase to accommodate the larger boats that now moor here. (*Author*)

Looking towards Rosewell's Boathouse and a distant Walton Bridge. Nearby Mount Felix was converted to a convalescent home during the First World War for New Zealand troops who had fought at Gallipoli. Some of these troops can be seen enjoying the Thames. (*Author*)

A popular place to relax and feed the swans in 2008, the boathouse is still there, albeit extended, and the towpath has been realigned. (*Author*)

Barges moored at Walton Wharf, date unknown. A wharf was thought to have existed here as early as the seventeenth century and was still marked on a 1920s Ordnance Survey map of this area along with gasworks, sawmills, farms, boathouses and a pavilion. The Anglers pub was built in 1870 and originally called Anglers Cottage; the first landlord described his job as 'fisherman'. (*Elmbridge Museum*)

The site of the former wharf has kept some familiar features including the Anglers pub and the former boathouse. Barge traffic no longer calls here as that trade has all but disappeared. Ducks, geese and swans are kept well fed by members of the public with food that can be bought nearby. (*Author*)

Under a 1924 Unemployment Relief Scheme, the backwater at Wheatley's Ait near Sunbury was widened, dredged and landscaped. Photographed from the location of the new weir, this view shows work well under way. (*Environment Agency*)

A 2007 view from the weir looking downstream with Wheatley's Ait on the right. According to a schedule of works for this scheme, the new weir was positioned on land once occupied by the bungalow Here we R. Three other bungalows were significantly altered during these works; Summer Haven, Cubbyhole and The Bung. Owners on both sides of the 18-metre channel also lost some land in the new contoured backwater arrangement aimed at improving flood relief. (*Author*)

Sunbury Lock Cut looking towards the older bridge crossing to Sunbury Church Ait, date unknown. To the right of the path is a long straight strip of land referred to locally as the 'ropewalk'. In 1813, this strip of land was rented to John Steel for making rope, yet he was refused permission to live on the site. Rope is made from hemp which has an explosive dust and perhaps it was this that caused the fire in Mr Steel's tar house here in 1821. (*Author*)

A 2007 view of Sunbury Lock Cut. The towpath here was found to be seriously undermined a few years ago and improvement works have been undertaken at a cost in the region of £300,000. The old ropewalk has all but gone and in its place is a road with a separate path for pedestrians. To the left of the view the Environment Agency have also installed numerous lights (for safety reasons) costing £400 each. When the author's father was lock keeper here he used a powerful torch. (*Author*)

A rare and early view looking downstream to old Sunbury Lock and house. The exact date of this view is unknown, but it is certainly from before 1926 when the second lock was built alongside this one. The house in this view was demolished in 1959. (*Environment Agency*)

A completely different view in 2008 with the 1926 lock alongside the earlier chamber. The first and much older City Lock was built in 1856 further upstream, close to the existing lock cut bridge and the old lock house. (*Author*)

Old Sunbury Lock photographed before 1926 from the top lock gates. When the author's father was lock keeper here in the late 1970s there was an ongoing dredging contract which had a semi-permanent conveyor belt running under the towpath. Spoil was offloaded from barges into a hopper feeding the conveyor belt which dropped the contents into waiting lorries. A plaintive cry of help was heard by the author's father who discovered the belt operator trapped by his hand between the spinning drum and the belt. It turned out that he was wearing gloves to protect his hands and had thrown stones under the drum to stop the conveyor belt slipping. His gloves caught and dragged his hand into the spinning drum and belt. Unfortunately, he was unable to reach the stop button. As a result of wearing gloves he lost his little finger, most of two other fingers and half the palm of his hand; all of which were ground away by the serrated drum. (*Author*)

Old Sunbury Lock in 2007, empty and quiet. Just visible on the left is the crest from the ivy-clad house in the previous view. There are discussions taking place about filling this lock in, such is the decline in traffic. (*Author*)

Passengers taking the ferry over to the 'Karsino' on Tagg's Island, date unknown. Tagg's Island was previously known as Walnut Tree Ait and Kent's Ait after the 1850 owner Francis Kent. Opened in 1913, the Karsino belonged to Fred Karno, famous for his circus. The hotel had tennis courts, a theatre, restaurant, bar, café and held concerts for up to 800 people at a time. (*Author*)

Houseboats moored at Tagg's Island in 2007. The Karsino was previously called Anglers Retreat and the Thames Riviera in 1928. There were numerous attempts to revive the fortunes of this venue, but it was eventually demolished in 1971. (*Author*)

A busy time at Molesey Lock with a steam launch, punts, canoes and a crowd of spectators. The dress suggests that this photograph was taken in the 1920s. At the 1895 Molesey Regatta, this lock recorded an astonishing 12,000 boats, 12 launches, 8 barges and issued over 1,200 tickets for the boat rollers. (*Author*)

Molesey Lock in 2007 on a sunny Sunday and quite a contrast from the busy scene in the previous view as the rollers are hardly ever used; they are now mainly occupied as an open storage area. (*Author*)

Looking upstream to Molesey Lock, taken from Hampton Court Bridge in about 1870 by Henry Taunt. In the seventh century Molesey was known as Mulesi or Mul's Island; around the time of Henry VIII it was called Mollsey, finally changing to the name we know today sometime around the eighteenth century. (*Oxfordshire County Council Photographic Archive*)

Over one hundred years later and the area around Molesey Lock bears no relation to the previous view. There are still boats for hire by Hampton Court Bridge, this time from Martin and Son, not Harry Tagg. There are still steps here in front of the former Thames Hotel as well as an advert for Whitbread Ales painted on the wall. (*Author*)

Looking downstream from Hampton Court Bridge to the Barge Walk. This 3-mile crescent of land took its present form in about 1701 when it was recast for King William III. It soon became a popular promenade when the new railway station opened in 1849. It was also a regular beach for the locals and visitors seen here, with plenty of boats let from T.R. Abnett and Sons. These numerous sheds were demolished in the late twentieth century as they were considered 'unsightly'. (*Mary Clarke Collection*)

Looking downstream from Hampton Court Bridge to the Barge Walk in 2008 and the view has dramatically changed owing to the fact that the previous image was taken from the pre-1933 bridge situated some 50 metres upstream. Turks have three piers where launches travel to and from Kingston and Richmond. Hire boats are available here but not on a cold February morning! (*Author*)

This view looking downstream from Kingston Bridge was probably taken before 1863 when the railway bridge was built. On the left is the Sun Hotel landing stage and it is a very busy day at the river. Note the horse taking a drink in the foreground. (*Author*)

A 2007 view from Kingston Bridge bears no resemblance to the packed shoreline of the previous view. To the right is a John Lewis department store along with Turks Town End Pier. On the left of the view modern apartments have been built on the former Gridley Miskin's Timber Yard, just upstream from the site of the earlier bridge. (*Author*)

Work in progress at Teddington Lock in 1903 – it was formally opened in June 1904. On an exceptionally high tide in 1906, it was possible for a tug to pass the lock without opening any of the lock gates! (*Environment Agency*)

An early morning photograph of Teddington Lock, February 2008. Maintenance work on the lock over the winter of 2007/8 included the installation of new steel lock gates and the lifting crane for this work may be seen in the background. (*Author*)

In 1934 when this photo was taken below Teddington Weir, there was a severe drought causing problems for these men. It is unclear exactly what they are loading or unloading from the flat; some men to the left of the view appear to be filling a wheelbarrow. Some of the Thames weir pools have had large concrete blocks deliberately sunk in them to mitigate the effects of scouring. (*Environment Agency*)

The last serious River Thames drought was in the summer of 1976. Water was so scarce at that time that huge back pumps were installed on Molesey Weir. When Teddington Weir was blown up by enemy action during the Second World War, laden barges were sunk across the breach while emergency repairs were carried out. The weir pool here has debris from that repair as well as large shoals. During the nesting season the lock keeper has to fend off attacking Canada geese to gain access to the weir. (*Author*)

Looking downstream from Richmond Bridge, certainly photographed after 1848 when the rail bridge in the view opened. Note the Thames sailing barges and punts in this view. (*Environment Agency*)

A 2007 view from Richmond Bridge is similar to the older view. Instead of the sailing barges there is a floating restaurant and most of the punts have gone. The building on the right is now a Young's pub, the White Cross. Many businesses are located under the promenade arches, including artists and boat builders. (*Author*)

Low tide at Strand on the Green photographed in the winter of 1902. In the distance is the temporary bridge crossing at Kew, erected while the new bridge was being completed. To the right of the view is the Pier House Steam Laundry Works, at one time the largest laundry in London. It only closed in 1973, owing to a lack of workers. Skulls dating back to 600 BC were found near here as well as some Roman pottery. In 1353, Strand on the Green was known as 'Stronde' possibly meaning shore. (*Chiswick Library*)

Low tide at Strand on the Green in 2007, although there is the obvious Kew Tower for a reference point, this image proved quite troublesome to photograph. Most of the waterfront buildings have gone including the Pier House Steam Laundry Works. Many of the modern dwellings on the right have half-sized doors and other unique flood defences. (*Author*)

BIBLIOGRAPHY

A Thames Companion by Mari Prichard & Humphrey Carpenter.
Domesday, the search for the roots of England by Michael Wood.
Thames Crossings by Geoffrey Phillips.
The Making of the Middle Thames by David G. Wilson.
The Royal Hundred of Cookham by Luke Over & Chris Tyrrell.
The Thames from source to tideway by Peter Chaplin.
The Thames Highway (Volume 1, General History) by F.S. Thacker.
The Thames Highway (Volume 2, Locks and Weirs) by F.S. Thacker.
The Thames Path by David Sharp.
The Thames, Record of a working waterway by David G. Wilson.

SOME INTERNET SITES

www.british-history.ac.uk
www.canaljunction.com
www.moleseyhistory.co.uk
www.portoflondon.co.uk
www.riverthamessociety.org.uk
www.thamespilot.org.uk
www.the-river-thames.co.uk
www.visitthames.co.uk
www.wikipedia.org

AUTHOR'S NOTE

During the compilation of this volume I endeavoured to take the modern photographs from the same spot as the original image. This was not always possible as changes over the last century made positive identification difficult. Sometimes it was necessary to climb trees and walls or hang precariously over the river to obtain the best possible view! I hope you enjoy my efforts. Some of these photographs will shortly be available as limited edition signed prints; please visit:
www.thamesphotos.co.uk